# Contents

| | |
|---|---|
| Preface | 1 |
| Introduction | 5 |
| Motherland | 6 |
| Failed Things | 8 |
|     Round 1 | 8 |
|     Round 2 | 10 |
|     Round 3 | 11 |
| Alphabet | 12 |
| Translation | 14 |
| Free Falling | 16 |
| Me, Myself and I | 18 |
| Meshki: Royal Black, Potato Sacks, i.e., Meaningmization | 20 |

# Preface

During the earliest stages of my life I recall having a fascination with visual media. Even before I learned to make sense of words I was deeply interested in imagery. I would make up stories based on the pictures I encountered, a tradition which I've carried to this day. As a child my parents and I would invest our leisure time visiting theaters, the opera and various museums. Both of whom valued aesthetic practices vastly throughout their lives and instilled within me a deep respect for all forms of art. I recall their interest in supporting emerging artists as a form of investment. I admired them for filling my life with endless still life paintings, even if I rarely had access to them as they were stored most of the time. Those intimate moments in which I was allowed to connect with these artworks, I felt a deep respect for my parents as collectors and the artists as creators. My first visit to an artist studio came when I was thirteen years old, I was fortunate to visit a renown member of the USSR's most prestigious artist association. Speaking to him was a surreal experience to say the least. Thus myself and my aesthetic queries and interests were born out of Moscow, Russia. During my childhood however, I traveled extensively and lived for prolonged periods of time all over the world: Algeria and Burundi in Africa, as well as Barcelona in Spain, Paris in France, as well as Munich and Frankfurt in Germany, until finally settling in the United States in 2010.

In a previous articulation of my professional self, I was a graphic artist, a web designer and an art director. I began the early stages of my college career exploring the graphic arts, and for years I sat in an office with countless other individuals

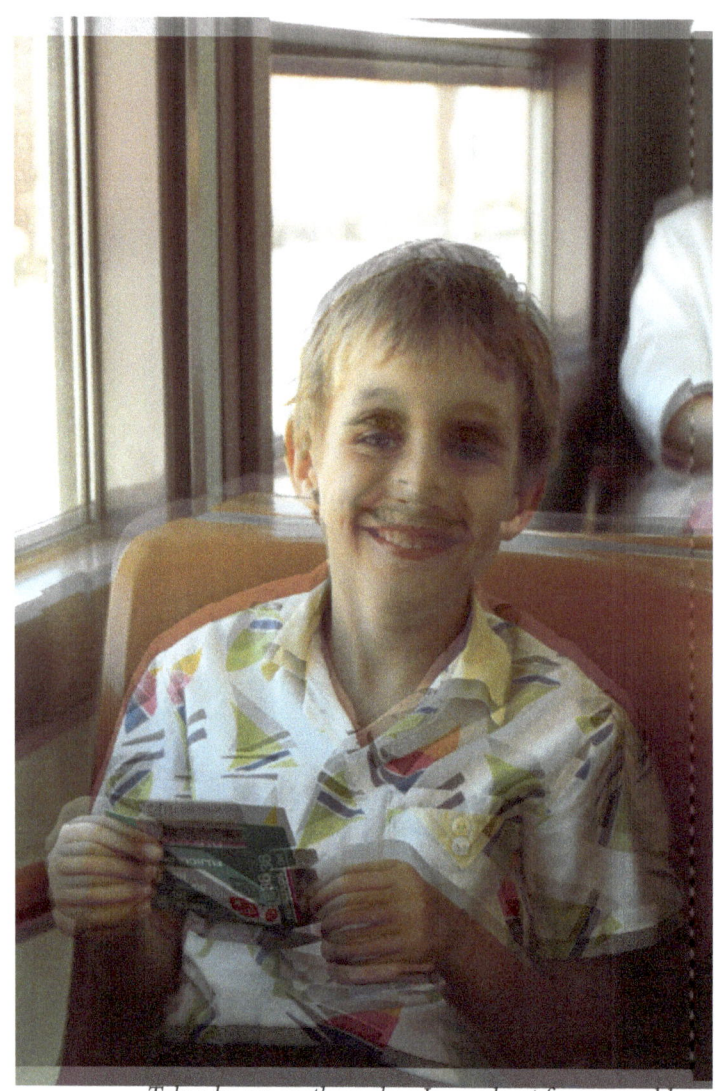

*Taken by my mother, when I was about five years old.*
*Taken by my mother, when I was about five years old.*

producing similar designs in infinite repetition. I thought this to be my life path. Lucky for me there was a photography studio next door. I quickly found myself taking extended breaks to speak to photographers, and wondered in an endless discovery. It was an escape for me then as it is now. Photography thus became a place of pure artistic expression. During my undergraduate work, photography transitioned into a craft; it became a set of skills used to enhance reality and create a desire. Not until one of my professors introduced me to alternative photographic techniques, did I indulge in the playfulness of the media, I learned yet again how to embrace unexpected results.

I value the process of creation itself. The gestures articulated toward the physical material in the developmental stages of production are a significant part of my modus operandi, where the finished artifacts become a witnessing vessels of an interaction between me and the material world. These articulations are rarely observed by the viewer, my conceptual essence thus permeates an object that is easy to consume by its end user. In my early days as an artist I was creating works that lacked any significant depth and often felt the yearn to seek a specialized audience in search of aesthetic understanding, yet found my creations too delicate.

As an artist I seek to encourage an audience to confront their preconceived ideas and overly generalized opinions. What interests me is how we as a society see the world. For instance, when we speak about directions, we commonly refer to North as up and South as down. An important matter as simple as geographical orientation is taken for granted every day, because centuries ago the Northern European cartographers who invented the antecedents to the modern map decided to put themselves above the rest of the world. Contemporarily, the confines of the internet gave birth to a meme that reads 'Australia is No Longer Down Under', text which is directly overlaid onto a south-up oriented map. Yet from outer space, Earth can be oriented in every direction possible. Nevertheless, we as a society have communally agreed that the world should be seen in a certain way. I think it's critical to be able to disagree with that premise, and to see and show the world in a way that might make people feel not comfortable.

My global perspective, childhood memories, interests and contemporary concerns currently converge on the digital realm. Just as Uda Barth creates in the confines of her own home, I turn to technology for inspiration as it can simultaneously be a form of entertainment, a social hub, a library, a shopping mall, and even an art studio. By acutely delving into technological channels I simultaneously immerse and isolate myself in their restrains, however am capable of accessing fractured segments of infinite data. This realm allows me the flexibility to explore culture and its perceptions of art, religion, fame, and countless other subjects that occupy my thoughts.

# Introduction

I was 29. Concord, California. Thanksgiving with friends. After dinner everyone played Catch Phrase. The goal for each player was to get their team to say the word suggested by previous team. One member of a team starts the timer and tries to get his or her team to guess the word. We were playing a third round, where a clue-giver had ten seconds to formulate a sentence describing a word. His team had one try and only twenty seconds to guess it. Time was on. The clue-giver spilled out: 'A place we end up after we die?' In my head I had the entire biblical story unveiling itself in one minute: Creation, Noah, Promised Land, Jesus, Jerusalem. And I knew the answer. I had no doubts. I was already thinking how elegantly the clue was put. It must be *Heaven*. The answer was given, and it was a correct one. It came as a shock to me that my answer was wrong. The correct answer was: Cemetery.

I was 29. And for the first time in my life I realized that I never before met people, who were brought up as atheists. All of my friends, even if they were agnostics or atheists, were brought up as Christians. And here I had a group of twenty individuals, who had no problem with the idea that after death we all go into the ground and nothing happens. They were as happy about life as anyone else I knew. They celebrated it as much as I did.

# Motherland

According to The Primary Chronicle written by Nestor the Chronicler, in 975 Vladimir the Great extended Russian monarchy, and in 988 established Christianity.[1] 998 years later I was baptized in a small Russian Orthodox Church. My introduction to the Christianity started with a traumatic experience. On the way to the church my mother's side of the family got finally reunited. They had a lot to talk about, and they were loudly arguing on the way. They forgot to mention an important part: What exactly is going to happen? Probably, for them it was obvious, but I never was baptized before or have never seen anyone being baptized. When the priest submerged me into the water, I was absolutely sure that he was trying to drown me, and that's the end of my life journey. I think for the entire country, when Vladimir the Great decided to establish Christianity it was like that day for me — a traumatic experience.

When the Soviet Union was established by the Bolsheviks in 1922, it was the constitutional organization which took over from the Russian Empire. One of the objectives was to eliminate the religion and substitute it with universal atheism[2]. The communist regime confiscated religious property, ridiculed religion, harassed believers, and propagated atheism in schools. In four years, 28 bishops and more than 1,200 priests were killed. Many more were persecuted. In schools we used to study

---

1 Taylor, W. C., C. S. Henry, and L. L. Smith. *A Manual of Ancient and Modern History*, New York: D. Appleton, 1851. Print.

2 Ramet, Sabrina P. *Religious Policy in the Soviet Union*. Cambridge: Cambridge UP, 1993. Print.

a famous quote by V.I. Lenin referring to Marx: 'Religion is the opium of the people.'[3] A transition to Marxist-Leninist Atheism was another traumatic experience for the country.

The transgenerational transmission of Holocaust trauma is well documented[4]. Even though it still remains a source of considerable controversy, I believe we can inherit other traumas through generations as well. Through my project I am seeking to understand better my own experiences and address a bigger issue.

---

3   Lenin, V. I. *About the attitude of the working party toward the religion. Collected works*, v. 17, p.41. Retrieved 2015-12-19.

4   Fossion, Pierre; Rejas, Mari-Carmen; Servais, Laurent; Pelc, Isy; Hirsch, Siegi. *Family approach with grandchildren of Holocaust survivors*. American Journal of Psychotherapy, Vol 57(4), 2003, 519-527.

# Failed Things                                         Round 1

Art is about failure. Every failure in art is a discovery. It's almost impossible to think of any failure related to drawing, painting, photograph, video, etc. You take a large format film camera and go outside to take a picture of a sunset. But a shutter doesn't fire right before the money shot should be captured. It's a mechanical failure. You can start being a paranoid android, who would check his gear thousand times before going out and still have accidents, failures, and make mistakes.

According to a story, Vasily Surikov was 19 years old, when he was working as a clerk in the provincial administration of the Yenisei in Krasnoyarsk, Russia. One day he drew a fly on a side of an official paper. The paper went to the governor Zamyatnin, who tried to catch it and was shocked to realize that it was drawn. Zamyatnin found a benefactor for young Surikov, who paid for his study at the St. Petersburg Academy of Arts. Later, Vasily Surikov became one of the best Russian painters of XIX century. One can see it as a mistake that transformed itself into a life-changing opportunity.

'If an angel is no more than a fly, then, conversely, a fly is an angel. Therefore, when the artist, following Mayakovsky's advice, ceases to draw an angel and begins to draw a fly, the result is an angel anyway.'[1]

Fortunately, writing about failure with a boring introduction, some random fact from Art History of Russia 101 and a metaphysical quote in the end was not a mistake. Jokes are on me.

---

1   Groys, Boris. *History Becomes Form: Moscow Conceptualism.* MIT Press, n.d. Web. 13 Sept. 2013.

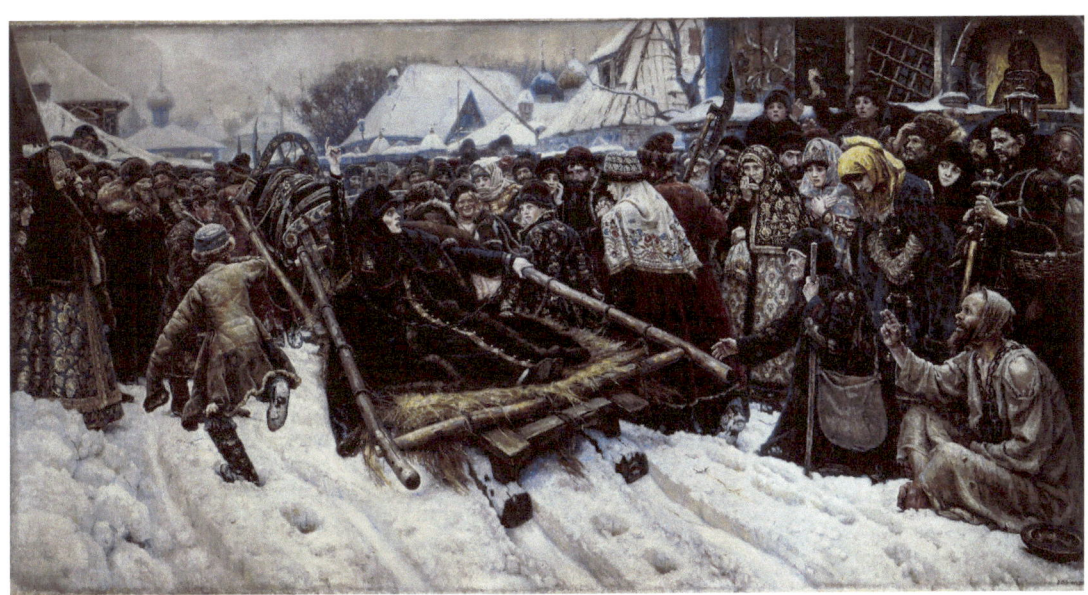

*Boyarina Morozova* by Vasily Ivanovich Surikov, 1887

*Whose fly is that?* by Ilya Kabakov, 1987

# Failed Things

## Round 2

*Fuckin feast for the eyes,*

*Believe now, beast killer arise,*

*In my opinion this dominion is mine*

*Banished, days gone away*[1]

A quote a day keeps a doctor away. Mistake, failure, error, accident. Helen Dunmore stated once: 'Reread, rewrite, reread, rewrite. If it still doesn't work, throw it away. It's a nice feeling, and you don't want to be cluttered with the corpses of poems and stories which have everything in them except the life they need.' How easy it is to use somebody else's voice? Why not write a poem from citations from other people?

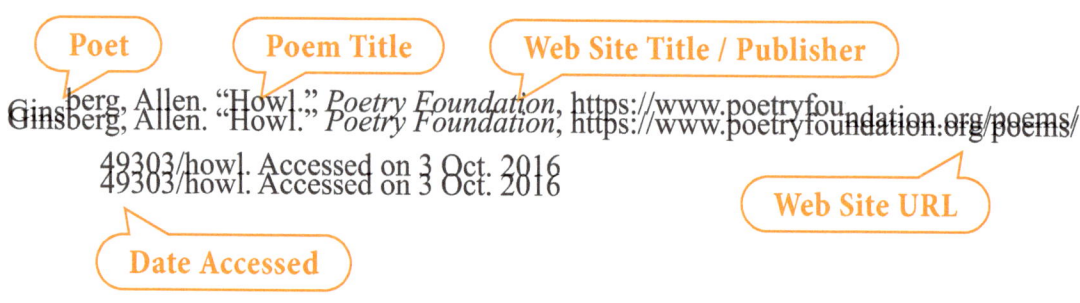

Ginsberg, Allen. "Howl." *Poetry Foundation*, https://www.poetryfoundation.org/poems/49303/howl. Accessed on 3 Oct. 2016

Execute a command. Poem. Poet Title. Web Site Title/Publisher. Web Site URL. Date accessed. Thank you. Bye.

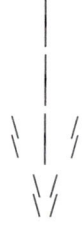

---

[1] Devildriver, These Fighting Words | LyricsMode.com. N.p., n.d. Web. 24 Apr. 2017.

# Failed Things

## Round 3

I am sitting across from her. She is waiting for empanadas. We are arguing about failure. She is saying that there is no such a thing as a mistake that she could learn from. I am bringing up an example with a child who was told that fire is hot, and he or she shouldn't touch it. I believe that eventually he or she still will touch something hot to make sure or prove to oneself that what parents say is truth. Or just learn from his or her own experience. We often equate mistakes with experiences and vice versa.

I don't know how to draw. Presumably, I do a lot of mistakes. But I enjoy doing what I don't know. If I would know exactly what I am doing, I would probably enjoy it less. My inner child is jumping from joy from discovering something new and previously unknown for myself. Each mistake is a success. Every deviation from expectations and logic moves me forward.

<html><head><title>Failed Things</title><body>Hello, World!</body></html>

'Hello, World!' is used in a sanity test to make sure that a computer language is correctly installed, and that the operator understands how to use it. Does operator know how to make mistakes? Does know how to get from point A to point B?

# Alphabet

A. Absorption, Abstraction, Anxiety, Annihilation

B. Bad, Broke, Beaten up, Bumpy

C. Complete, Corrected, Compulsive, Contradiction

D. Death, Dead, Destruction, Determination

E. Eruption, Erection, Enormous, Empathy

F. Fuck, Fuck, Fuck, Fuck

G. Global, Ghetto, Grumpy, Grandpa

H. Horny, Humble, Home, Harakiri

I. Irony, Iconic, I, Impulsive

J. Joke, Jerk, Jumbo, Jack

K. Kill, King, Kick, Kolkhoz

L. Lame, Lotto, Loyal, Literature

M. Moscow, Me, Migraine, Menstruation

N. Nothingness, Notorious, No, Never

O. Opium, Opposition, Opportunity, Oscar

P. Poop, Pilot, Pee, Pillow

Q. Question, Quintessence, Quick, Quantic

R. Reason, Rational, Reverse, Reform

S. Submarine, Superb, Suicide, Sorrow

T. Tilt, Total, Twerk, Tamagotchi

U. Universe, Universal, University, United

V. Victory, Video, Vodka, Vendetta

W. What, Why, Who, Where

X. X-Mas, X-Men, X-Large, Xerox

Y. Yolo, Year, Yesterday, Yolk

Z. Zorro, Zombie, Zap, Zip

# Translation

I go there every morning. I open a door and enter one hundred and twenty-six square feet of sacred headspace located close to my heart. I dive into ambitions, emotions and regrets. On my desk, I see a map for a quick and easy return to personal. I remember, when I was a kid my grandfather was holding my hand firmly passing by the dumpsters of our neighborhood, peaking inside and excavating treasures from other worlds. These days I don't have his guidance any longer. I am left on my own seeking for the meaning of things that used to mean something for somebody else. They create a narrative that eventually manifests itself onto the wall. Objects form sentences, sentences make paragraphs. Everything is according to what he taught me, when I was five. Nothing is everything. Everything is emptiness. Emptiness is a complete darkness.

"The intentionality of display lies in opening up an active space between object and label that propels the spectator in a 'shuttling process', back and forth, hither and thither, between culturally informative causes and visually interesting objects."[1]

---

1  Bhabha, Homi K. *Beyond the Pale: Art in the Age of Multicultural Translation*. New York: Whitney Museum of American Art, 1993. Print.

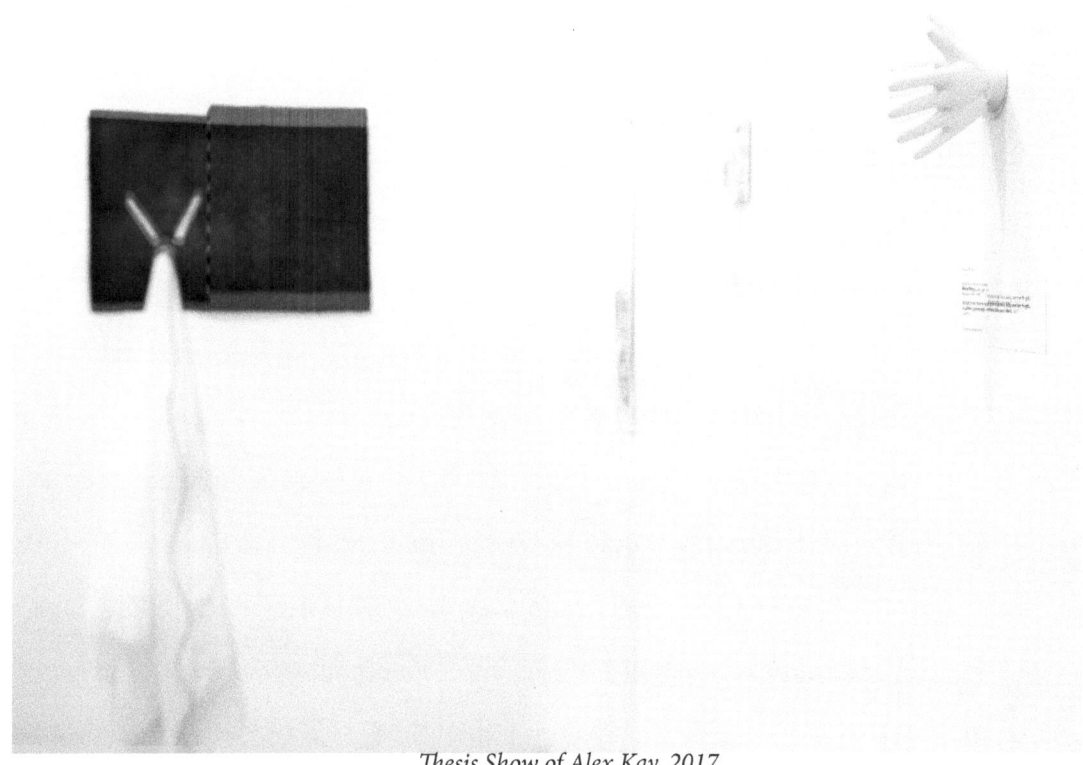

*Thesis Show of Alex Kay, 2017*
*Thesis Show of Alex Kay, 2017*

# Free Falling

Dumpster diving. Binning. Canning. Dumpster-munching. Totting. Skipping. Skip Diving. Skip salvage. Curb shopping. Trash picking. Street scavenging. Scrapping. But not gleaning (food).

My grandpa was born in August 19, 1921. A little more over a year after he was born, the Soviet Union was formed with the unification of the Russian, Transcaucasian, Ukrainian, and Byelorussian republics. Those were hard transitional times for Russian people. During his childhood he was playing with whatever he could find. A stick and a rock are the best toys that would outlast all of us. But they are not always enough. He went through the World War II, received best education and after years of diplomatic service, he still was playing with things he would excavate from nearest trash bins. My grandpa could see beyond ordinary in things. Moreover, he was a healer. He could repair an old motorized child's car, rebuild a part of a commode, sew back in a teddy bear's hand. My grandma never understood him fully. She thought of his hobby as of some kind of mental disorder, and she shamed him.

I am not as handy as my grandpa. I live in different times: we stopped repairing things. It's cheaper to buy a new item and throw away an old one. Most items are made to be replaced in a three-five year cycle. Many household electric devices do not have a repair manual. Enthusiasts are buying antiquated car repair manuals to understand, how to repair their vehicles in an efficient and inexpensive fashion.

The objects around us became impersonal. My toothbrush in a cup on a sink in my bathroom is not mine anymore. Now, it's a disposable element of my environment, I don't think of it as mine, I have no personal connection to it. I have to replace it every other month, and I have a dozen of them in a drawer under my sink. I don't hold on to things as I used to, when I was a kid discovering things from trash with my grandpa and many uses they could possibly have.

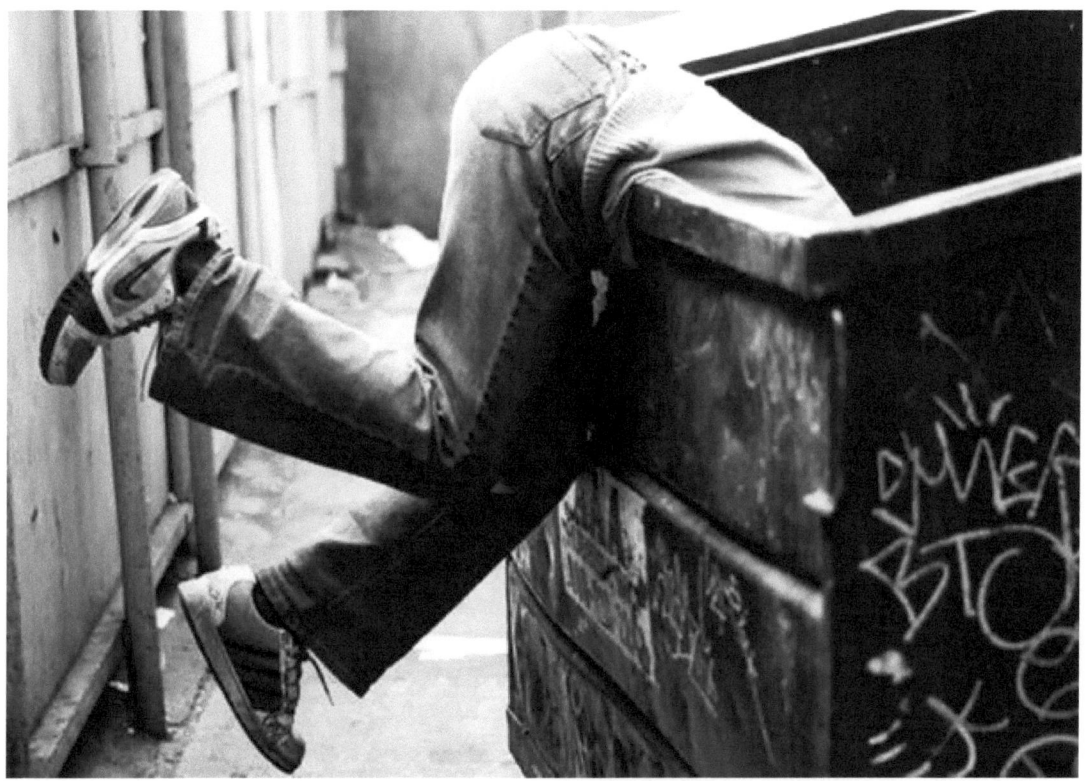

*From The Top 5 Things To Do in Montreal[1], Unknown Photographer*

---

1  Fidel, Andy. *The Top 5 Things To Do in Montreal: November 27 to December 8*. Concordia University. N.p., 27 Dec. 2014. Web. 24 Apr. 2017.

# Me, Myself and I

Q: What are the things on the walls?
A: Objects and labels/captions for them.

Q: What is Mickey Mouse?
A: Mickey Mouse is a character and a mascot of The Walt Disney Company. Most famous animated anthropomorphic mouse in the world since 1928. I met people, who believe in Mickey Mouse as strongly as one may believe in Jesus or Allah.

Q: Why there is a hole?
A: There is always a hole.

Q: Is it really a hole?
A: Yes, it is really a hole.

Q: What is an object?
A: An object is an anchor to start a conversation. Some objects are interchangeable. Others are not.

Q: Why people take selfies with those objects?
A: I don't know. Maybe it's a good sign.

Q: Do people read what text says?
A: Some of them do. Some of them give up after one-three-four reads.

Q: Do people believe in what text says?
A: I tried to challenge the relationship between a label and an object. I was interested to investigate institutional power.

Q: Is text important?
A: Yes, I see text as a work. An object is an element that supports it.

Q: What is language?
A: "Any system of formalized symbols, signs, sounds, gestures, or the like used or conceived as a means of communicating thought, emotion, etc."[1]

Q: Is there any relationship between an object and a text?
A: Yes, it's a binary relationship. A group of an object and a text can be seen as a letter that forms a word; as a word that forms a sentence; as a sentence that forms a paragraph. Letters, words, and sentences can be moved around to convey different ideas.

Q: Is there a narrative?
A: Yes.

---

[1] "Language." Dictionary.com, www.dictionary.com/browse/language. Accessed 20 Apr. 2017.

# Meshki: Royal Black, Potato Sacks, i.e., Meaningmization

~~Meaning, definition, sense, explanation, denotation, connotation, interpretation, nuance.~~

I would like to emphasize nuance for 2 seconds. My grandpa was born on August 19, 1921. A little more than a year after he was born, the Soviet Union was formed. I was born right after the Iranian Revolution. A subtle difference for it really sounds prettier for the animal that therefore I am. He went through World War II, received the best education and after years of diplomatic service, he was still playing with things he could excavate from the trash. And I survived the Iran–Iraq war. I would like to start naked in the first place, please don't get me wrong: by the word naked I am not interested in nudity. My grandpa was a dumpster diver at heart. Today I'm so weak, so in pain, bleeding, almost invisible for I was called a woman by Khodah (Allah), who plans to speak endlessly. He was the person who introduced me to the idea of looking beyond what things might be, and the meaning they can bring to the table.

Walter Benjamin does not believe in true translation; neither do I, therefore I say it in Farsi: '*Parvaz ra be khater bespar parandeh mordanist.*'[1] Meshki in Farsi means Royal Black, whereas in Russian it means Potato Sacks.

Yesterday. I do not believe in yesterday anymore.

Tomorrow. I do not believe in tomorrow anymore.

---

1   Translation: «Remember the fly for the bird is mortal», Forough Farokhzad

*Alex Kay was a part of Meshki Collective since 2016. Through research, video, sculpture, photography, wall painting, and various objects he was creating environments that submerged viewers in a flood of experiences, which addressed critical thinking. His works talked through the paradoxes of migration, identity, philosophy and politics.*

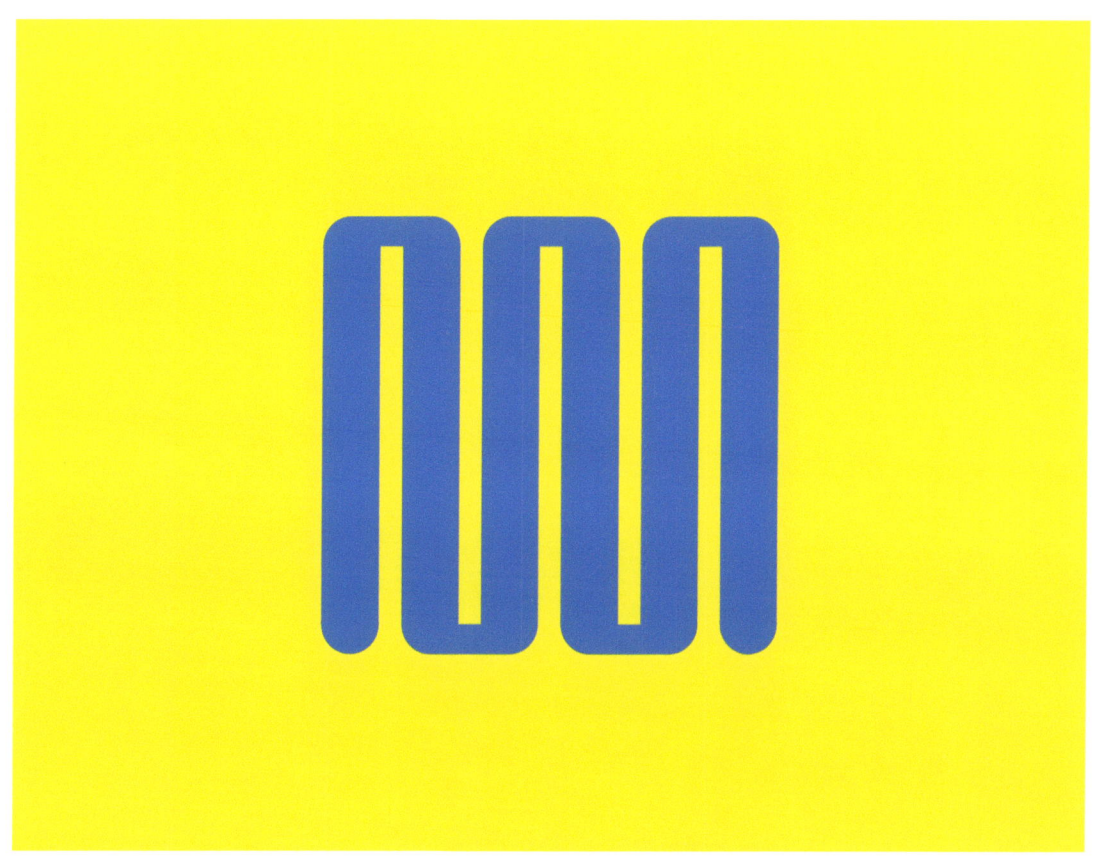

*Meshki Collective Logo, 2017*

© 2017 Published for Thesis II Class, Instructor Benjamin Weissman.
© 2017 Published for Thesis II Class, Instructor Benjamin Weissman.
Written by Alex Kay. Dedicated to all who still read.
Written by Alex Kay. Dedicated to all who still read.

www.ingramcontent.com/pod-product-compliance
Lightning Source LLC
Chambersburg PA
CBHW051943210526
45473CB00006B/2357